Who Stole the Fez, Moors or Shriners?

© *2014 CALIFA MEDIA PUBLISHING* ™

Written By

Grand Sheik Brother Kudjo Adwo El
Moorish Science Temple of America
Subordinate Temple #5 – Toronto
Canaanland

Edited By

Sheikess Tauheedah S. Najee-Ullah El
Moorish Science Temple California, Inc.

Who Stole the Fez, Moors or Shriners?

© 2014, 2020

Califa Media Publishing ™
Park Forest, Illinois

Written by
Grand Sheik Kudjo Adwo El
Moorish Science Temple of America
Subordinate Temple #5 - Toronto
Canaanland

Edited by
Sheikess Tauheedah S. Najee-Ullah El
Moorish Science Temple California, Inc.

ISBN-13: 978-1-952828-81-2

All Rights Reserved. Without Prejudice. No Part Of This Book May Be Reproduced Or Transmitted In Any Form By Any Means, Electronic, Photocopying, Mechanical, Recording, Information Storage Or Retrieval System Unless For The Liberation Of Minds And Gaining Knowledge Of Self.

Califa Media®
A Moorish Guide Publishing Company
califamedia.com
All Rights, Remedies & Liberties Reserved

Table of Contents

Moorish American Prayer _____ i

Prologue _____ 1

1. Introduction _____ 2

2. The Order of Degrees _____ 3

3. Symbology _____ 4

4. Moabites and Moslems _____ 10

5. Operaziona Colomba _____ 12

6. Ottoman Influence _____ 16

7. The Moghul Empire _____ 18

8. South East Asia _____ 19

9. Etymology and Form _____ 20

10. The Fez in the MHT of S and MST of A _____ 26

11. Fez-Wearing Imposters _____ 28

12. Prophet Noble Drew Ali was not a Mason _____ 36

Works Cited _____ 40

Index _____ 42

Other Titles Available from Califa Media® _____ 43

Moorish American Prayer

ALLAH, the Father of the Universe, the Father of Love, Truth, Peace, Freedom and Justice. ALLAH is my protector, my guide, and my Salvation by night and by day, through His Holy Prophet DREW ALI (Amen)

Prologue

"The defeat and enslavement of the Moabite/ Moorish Nation in the Western Hemisphere is the most secret history in all public literature! Both the history and culture is kept from public consciousness as much as possible by the ruling Colonial States and their European citizen subjects."

Moors Order of the Roundtable Civic Lesson #5
Taj Tarik Bey

"The institution of slavery, which had long since died out in the rest of Western Europe, had here survived for a number reasons, especially because of the continuing wars with the Moors, which had lasted until the year of the discovery of America. (Tannenbaum 1992).

1. Introduction

The Ancient Arabic Order of the Nobles of the Mystic Shrine, commonly known as Shriners and abbreviated A.A.O.N.M.S. was established in 1867 by William J. Florence. It is said that Florence, along with a Dr. Walter M. Fleming, M.D., made a trip to the **Old World** and there secured useful information for the introduction and establishment of the Shrine. It is also said that it was Ali Ibn Ibi Talib, son-in-law and cousin of the Prophet Muhammad who taught the "Mystics" of this Shrine. On June 16, 1871, Dr. Fleming, assisted by Brother Florence, conferred Degrees upon four Knights Templar and seven members of Aurora Grata Consistory. While the Shriners, known as Moslem (Moorish) Sons, perhaps will argue their ritual represents the highest aspect of represents the highest aspect of Speculative Masonry, it is designed to teach moral lessons and further define principles of spirituality, as well as their constant quest to know The Deity by all **His** attributes. It must be noted there is also Operative Masonry. Obviously Shriners did not overstand the high science that Moors brought them because they still recognize the Deity or Higher Power as **He,** when the truth is there is no masculine creative energy in the universe, only **feminine.** Freemason Moslem sons realized that the power was in the **wombman** and the Moabite Nation – from which the Moorish Nation came out of – was a matriarchal society.

2. The Order of Degrees

Founded in Mexico in 1945, **The Order of Quetzalcoatl** was based upon a Mexican legend that depicts the struggle between the forces of good and evil. This order is composed of Shrine Masons who have distinguished themselves in their service to their respective temples. The physical foundation of Freemasonry exists under a charter issued by the Grand Lodge. Lodges are informally linked and offer different service and achievement programs. All lodges offer three basic degrees which are achieved through service and learning: Entered Apprentice, Fellow Craft, and Master Mason. Groups of advanced Masons confer as many as 30 additional degrees. These 30 additional degrees is how they arrive at 33 degrees of Freemasonry, but in reality it only has three degrees. These three degrees metaphysically are the Base, Navel and Solar plexus Chakras. The 33 degrees are the spine, in which the serpentine fire climbs in order for these "Moslem sons" to become enlightened or ILLUMINATED. Why would these Europeans call their order Arabic, Ancient or even Moslem when they were not the originators of these titles?

"Secret societies have been in existence at least since the date of the earliest known writings. Some have served utilitarian ends, others speculative; some have been visible, others invisible, except to government information services, which have always been aware of their existence. Each has based its existence on a secret, the secret of its mystery, purpose, direction, ritual or, more generally, its organization. Ultimately, what has at all times and in all places distinguished secret societies from other associations is that the former are organized in a manner parallel to, but often above, official forms of government, whatever those forms may be."

(Laliberte 2006)

3. Symbology

We can see clearly that the image of the wombman on the Shriners crest is a Melanite. It is also clear that the crescent and star is an Islamic symbol, not Christian. The Scimitar sword is displayed above her head to show she has been beheaded and continues to be, and in the place of a pendant is what could be the 5 point green star of the Moorish red flag. The crescent and star together represent Allah, or the Cosmos. This is supposed to be a secret to keep Hiram Abiff in a shallow grave.

The secret of these fraternal orders, as Bro Ashra Kwesi, Dr. Malachizodok El and other Master Ma-Sons or Moslem Sons Fathers teach us is that ALL Shriner/ Masonic attire, rituals, passwords, handshakes/gestures have some kind of origin with the founders of civilization, Melanin beings or so called "black people". The true Ma Star builders were the Melanin beings from Al Kebulan, Mu-Atlantis and Al Moroc who build the miraculous, colossal pyramids and other structures of the ancient world.

The definition of a mason is a person who builds or works with stone or brick, another "secret" of the societies as we know our ancient forefathers were the first masons. During the middle ages, we find the word free mason defined as a member of a guild of skilled itinerant masons. The modern use of the term free mason or mason refers directly to an international secret fraternity who are Free AND Accepted. The original Mason was a worker, or a slave, so the freemasons separated themselves from these workers by calling their fraternity free, differentiating themselves from the slaves.

In early free masonry, acceptance into the Lodge came when you were selected to join, as explained in the earlier account of Dr. Fleming and Mr. Florence conferring Degrees upon four Knights Templar and seven members of Aurora Grata Consistory. These men were actually usurpers of a culture so powerful, yet so easy to steal since the "black man" is/ was dead. Ignorance is key to the whole freemasonry idea developing without fear of interference. The followers of Master Potentates are being led blindly through secrets, phrases and dues while being oblivious of the ability of elevated consciousness that is supposed to be gained in these orders. It must be noted: Potentate means Sultan!! Hiram Abiff, during the Third Degree of Free Masonry, is portrayed by the newly initiated Third Degree Freemason. Abiff was a man of

Tyre, the capital of Ancient Phoenicia, Grand Master builder of Solomon's Temple and knower of the "secrets of the Master Mason". Upon the completion of the Temple, according to Masonic legend, Abiff agreed to reveal the "secrets" and the name of God to fellow-crafts, in that they could go forth and earn wages as Masters. The idea was that the fellow crafts who worked on the Temple were to receive as compensation the secrets of the Master Mason. However, a plot was formed to compel Abiff to reveal the secrets. He was confronted by three ruffians at the East gate, South gate and West gate of the Temple where they demanded of Abiff, "Your life or the secrets." To this Abiff replied, "My life you can have, my integrity NEVER." Failing to acquire the secrets by threat, the first ruffian assaults Abiff with his working tool and Abiff staggers to the next gate. This happens three times at each of the three gates by each of the three ruffians. Employing the Entered Apprentice and Fellow-craft grips, King Solomon himself tries to raise Abiff but is unsuccessful.

King Solomon was finally able to raise Abiff with the Lion Paw grip, the so called REAL grip of the Master Mason. This is what Free Masons now call "being raised from a dead level to the living perpendicular". The King embraces Abiff on the five points of fellowship, foot to foot, knee to knee, breast to breast, hand to back, and mouth to ear.

"It was the single object of all the ancient rites and mysteries practiced in the very bosom of pagan darkness...to teach the immortality of the soul. This is the great design of the third degree of Free Masonry. This is the scope and aim of its ritual. The Master Mason represents man, when youth, manhood, old age, and life itself have passed away as fleeting shadows, yet raised from the grave of iniquity and quickened into another and better existence."- (Teixeira dos Santos M.M. n.d.)

Many Moorish Adepts, like C.M Bey in Clock of Destiny II, delve into the hidden mysteries that go "over the head" of the so called Master Masons of these Lodges. The 360 Degree Master Ma-Son Free Moorish American teaches,

"King Solomon is the Earth which contains all of the elements, wealth and forces of Nature. Hiram Abiff is the Sun, which marks the months, seasons, signs and the measurement of time and space during the earth's

annual revolution of 360 Degrees. The Grand Master is the "Fall" season. The Fatal Blow is December 21st or January 1st. Here the cold weather strikes its fatal blow on plant life. The approaching grip of the spring season against the winter season is referred to as "the grip of the Lions Paw", meaning the spring season has raised plant life from its "death bed" of frozen Earth to a "living perpendicular". (Bey n.d.)

In the early 1900's Prophet Noble Drew Ali graduated from the school of Islamism. Elder George G.M James tells us in his book, *Stolen Legacy*, that the Moors were **the custodians of Ancient Egyptian Mystery system**. (James 1992). Upon attaining the highest degree of knowledge of self and making his Hajj to Mecca, Noble Drew Ali returned to America with his holy or sacred free National name, El Hajj Sharif Abdul Ali. Noble Drew Ali /Sharif Abdul Ali was not a Mason, he was a Moslem and The Prophet of Islam in America.

"The Grip of the Entered Apprentice or BOAZ is made by pressing the thumb against the top of the first knuckle-joint of the fellow Mason, the fellow Mason also presses his thumb against the first Mason's knuckle. The name of this grip is "Boaz". (Roynayne 2007).

Masonry is universal – the true meaning of which is revival of Ancient Melanin Mysteries of Thought – are to be known only by the "adepts" of Free Masonry. The exoteric or apparent was for followers and the hidden true meanings or esoteric teachings were/are known to the small elite group of Masons in the Adept circles of Free Masonry.

555 Eastern Blvd, Montgomery, AL 36117

4. Moabites and Moslems

It is a historic fact that there was a Nation of people called Moabites from the land of Moab. Ruth the Moabitess has her own book in the Bible where she and her mother in-law Naomi, went from Moab to Bethlehem. In the history, Boaz bought Ruth the Moabitess since he was kinsman to Naomi's husband and a man of wealth.

Prophet Noble Drew Ali teaches in the Circle 7 Koran that the Moorish ARE descendants of the Ancient Moabites.

"The Moabites from the land of Moab received permission from the Pharaohs of Egypt to settle and inhabit North-West Africa: they were the founders and are the true possessors of the present Moroccan Empire."
(Noble Drew Ali 1928)

In 711 AD, barely one hundred years after the establishment of Islam, the Moors crossed from Northern Africa into Europe and conquered most of Spain. Many of the anti-Catholic

Christians and Jews residing in Spain during Moorish rule did not see the invasion as a totally bad thing as the Moors showed greater religious tolerance more than did the Catholics. Additionally, the Moors made many improvements to European society that was, at that time, on a downward spiral. The Moors brought with them a rich culture and scholarship that was sorely lacking in Medieval Christian society and missing even today in some parts of the world. Arriving with translations of the Higher Learning Institution of KMT (Egypt), the Moors established robust institutions of learning and enormous, well-stocked libraries. They set about improving and instituting agriculture, astronomy, architecture, science and mathematics. They called their new landholding Al-Andalus.

"It was inevitable that the two peoples would teach one another; the Moors, it seemed, had much more to teach the Spaniards. Ironwork produced in Castile and Andalucia developed in an entirely different way due to the influence of the Moorish artists in the area. Besides being influenced by their designs, the Spanish blacksmiths were also influenced by their work in other metals." (Hacienda Home Style 2008)

When the Moors first entered Spain, they made no attempt to force Christians nor Jews to convert to their way of life; Islam (Peace). Their holy book, the Koran, grants religious liberty and the protection of person and property to Christians and Jews. Moors were too complacent in their dealings with their enemies, so, some 700 years after their arrival in Europe, the Catholics attacked from the north and took over the whole of Spain. By 1492, they terrorized the Moors for hundreds of years, resulting in forced conversion to Catholicism or expulsion from the country. Those found to be not "Catholic enough" were subjected to torture in the Spanish Inquisition. There were Jews and Muslims living in Spain during Columbus' preparation for his historical voyage to the Americas.

5. Operaziona Colomba

An important historic fact regarding the "discovery of the Americas" was that King Ferdinand of Castile and Queen Isabella of Aragon gave Columbus permission to pursue his plans for the expedition only after the Fall of Granada. **Stolen Moorish wealth** was used to finance Columbus.

"On August 3rd, when Columbus set sail to cross the ocean, the harbors and waterways of Spain were clogged with ships taking the exiled Jews to North Africa, Portugal, Italy, and the Ottoman Empire. These three major events of 1492, the fall of Granada, the expulsion of the Jews, and Columbus's expedition, were not unrelated. The war against the Muslims was very costly, and there wasn't enough money in the treasury to finance both the war and the voyage across the Atlantic. The funds came from the booty taken from the Moors when Granada fell, and from loans made to the king and queen by financiers who were Jews and conversos; that is, Jews who had converted to Christianity." (Altabe 1992).

Moslems/Mohammedans/Moors who refused to convert faced penalties including as death, exile and imprisonment for adhering to Islam. These Moorish converts were known as Moriscos. However, many Moriscos or "little Moors" continued to practice as crypto– Muslims. Muslims were experiencing a revitalization of their culture and religion among the Moriscos. In the faraway Ottoman Empire, one ruler extended an immediate welcome to the persecuted Jews of Spain and "little Moors;" he was the Sultan Bayazid II (1481-1512).

The Spanish crown sought to expel both Muslims and Jews from newly conquered Spanish lands. In 1464, after the crusade against the Fell Spirits (known as demons in ancient religions) further polarized public opinion against spirit kind and the tainted races, Grand Inquisitor Tomas de Torquemada launched a vicious campaign to purge Spain, France and Italy of all magic-users. Torquemada brought thousands of suspected wizards before the Inquisition to stand trial for suspicion of using heretical magic. Conditions would never improve for those born with visible marks of sorcery: as the tainted races would be subjected to night-time raids of their homes by the Inquisition, and countless trials and interrogations.

In 1567, Phillip II of Spain increased pressure by issuing an order that required Moriscos to give up their Moslem/Moorish names and traditional Moslem/Moorish dress code. This is when the Moors lost their National headwear, the fez. It is alleged that Philip issued this decree not only for himself to usurp power, but it was mainly so the intent of provoking an unstoppable rebellion, so the Moriscos could be destroyed or expelled. It was during this period that Ottoman Turkey emerged as the dominant Muslim power in the Mediterranean Sea. There were increasing clashes between Turkey and Castile. Phillip II of Spain, fearing the Moriscos of Granada might aid a potential Turkish invasion of Spain, in 1568 had Muslims forcibly converted to Catholicism, resulting in the Alpujarra Uprising. The Morisco Revolt was a rebellion by the remnants of the Spanish/Moorish/Moslem Christian converts in Granada against the Kingdom of Castile. The revolt was planned by Ferag ben Ferag, a descendant from the royal house of Granada, and Diego Lopez ben Abu. They ascertained the disposition of the inhabitants of the Alpujarras – where the best stand could be made against the royal forces – solicited aid from the kings of North Africa, and persuaded the local bandits to embrace their cause.

The Spanish crown finally succeeded in expelling the remaining Moslem population in 1610; most of the refugees/P.O.W's made their way to lands controlled by the Ottoman Empire or to North Africa. The Spanish inquisition did not disappear but instead shifted its focus from the Morisco expulsions to the Jewish expulsion for the remainder of the 17th century. The era between 1478 and 1600 was the most active of the Spanish Inquisition, but it was not abolished until 1834 during the reign of Isabel II.

"The Altain Turks (Blue Turks/Moors), were subjects and served as blacksmiths for them." This geometric form of Moorish influence on Spanish ironwork remained evident until after the re-conquest. Its staying power is due in part to the fact that Spaniards and Moors worked side-by-side when designing and building Christian buildings.

6. Ottoman Influence

Sultan Mahmud II had originally introduced the fez to the Ottoman Empire's dress code in 1826 as a symbol of feudalism (military service). The fez ("Fes" in Turkish) was banned in 1925, and Turkish men were encouraged to wear European attire. The Ottoman Empire also known by its contemporaries as the Turkish Empire or Turkey was an Empire that lasted from 1299–1923 when it was succeeded by the Republic of Turkey.

Founded by Osman I, from which the name Ottoman is derived, the Ottoman Empire controlled much of South Eastern Europe and North Africa at the height of its power between the 16th–17th centuries. Osman I extended the frontiers of Ottoman settlement towards the edge of the Byzantine Empire. The Byzantine Empire and Eastern Roman Empire are conventional names used to describe the eastern portion of the Roman Empire during the Middle Ages. Centered on its capital of Constantinople, it was referred to by its inhabitants and neighboring nations simply as the Roman Empire, the Empire of the Romans. Osman I moved the Ottoman capital to Bursa and shaped its early political development.

Osman I was given the nickname "Kara" (which means "black" in modern Turkish,) and was admired as a strong and dynamic ruler long after his death, as evident in the centuries-old Turkish phrase, "may he be as good as Osman." Among Muslims of South Asia/Asia Soor/Africa, the fez is known as the Rumi Topi ("Roman cap") due to the hands it has passed through after the Moors expulsion from Spain. It was a symbol of Islamic identity and showed the Indian Muslims support for the Khilafat (Caliphate), headed by the Ottoman Emperor. Later, the fez became associated with the Muslim League, the political party which eventually created the country of Pakistan.

The Muslim League, was a political party in British India  that developed into the driving force behind the creation of Pakistan as a Muslim state on the Indian subcontinent. Late veteran Pakistani politician **Nawabzada Nasrullah Khan** was one of the few people in Pakistan who wore the fez until his death in 2003.

The Fez or Tarbush were also worn by Egyptian diplomats abroad. This requirement almost caused the breakdown of relations between Egypt and Turkey when, on the occasion of the  9th anniversary of the proclamation of the Turkish republic (October 29, 1932), **Abdel Malek Hamza Bey**, Egypt's envoy to Ankara, appeared at the Ankara Palace Hotel wearing his tarbush. Just like a flag, the tarbush was a national emblem. It was used at the Egyptian court, in the civil service, by the army and the police. Some officers wore it with a dashing slant, silken tassel flying in the breeze.

Crown Prince of Egypt and Sudan, Mohammed Ali Tewfik, wore it in a manner defying gravity, looking as if it would topple over at any moment. Others wore it as though it were a column, sweating profusely beneath it. Its shape was described in a 1937 English editorial as esthetically and basically inferior to European hats.

> "The practical advantages that the hat has over the tarbush is that the tarbush offers very little defense against the sun, its long chimney-pot length makes it a convenient victim of any random gust of wind, and in time of rain it has to be mollycoddled and swathed in its owner's handkerchief in case it should come to harm."

7. The Moghul Empire

The Muslim Mughal Empire ruled most of India from its capitol Delhi from the early 16th century, but after a major decline, its last power base in northern India was broken by the British in the 19th century. The Mughal Empire was an Islamic imperial power of the Indian subcontinent which began in the early 1500s, ruled most of the subcontinent by the late 17th and early 18th centuries, and ended in the mid-19th century.

The Mughal Emperors were Turko-Mongol. Turco-Mongol or Turko-Mongol is a word that has been used in history in reference to people or culture derived from Turkic People and the Mongols, hence "Turkic-Mongol."

8. South East Asia

The Khmer Empire was the largest in South East Asia located in what is now Cambodia. Its greatest legacy is Angkor, a sprawling temple complex built in the 12th Century. Roland Burrage Dixon wrote that the Khmers were physically "marked by distinctly short stature, dark skin, curly or even frizzy hair, broad noses and thick Negroid lips." (Dixon 1923). Angkor is a Khmer term meaning "city" and comes from the Sanskrit *nagara*. Nagas were the melanated Asians who can raise their kundalini energy, known as the *serpentine fire*.

Buddha statue of Angkor Wat wearing the fez

In Indonesia, the country with the biggest Muslim population in the world, fez is a part of the local culture itself. Fez is called "Peci" in Indonesian. The Peci is black in colour with a more ellipse shape and sometimes decorated with embroideries. Malaysian

Malay men are also seen wearing it as part of the local culture, and it is better known as "Songkok" in Malaysia. The peci is used in various ceremonies mostly religious and also in formal occasions by government officials.

9. Etymology and Form

Ancient Egyptians Wearing the Fez

"The fez, which Nobles of the Mystic Shrine of North America have the privilege and honor of wearing, has been handed down through the ages as one of the most significant of all headdresses. The fez derives its name from the place where it first was manufactured commercially, the holy city of Fez, in Morocco". (Jamil Shrine Temple n.d.)

The original term, fez, is Arabic word written **Faa'sur raa's**. Another source includes **Al Faas, *"the constellation of ursa minor"*** which takes you in to what the Moors called Zudiacus; the ancient zodiac studies of Moorish constellation mapping and tracking stars which they learned from the Egyptian Mystery schools.

Ursa minor.

The constellation having the shape of a ladle, with Polaris at his tips of its handle also called the little bear from Latin *minor* meaning little or lesser, and *ursa* meaning bear. The North Star (a common name for Polaris) was used by the great Moors for navigation between Africa and "the land of the frogs," an ancient reference to America. This star was also used by Moors under captivity (slavery) to escape north to "Khent," the Egyptian name source for the Iroquois tribal confederation name, Canadaigwa, [Kah-yeh-nah-da-ee-gah-wah], which is now CANADA, the corporate nation state. The Moors, especially of Timbuktu, were known to be the greatest sea farers, even teaching the Vikings how to build ships and sail the seas. The story of *Sinbad and the Eye of the Tiger*, was one movie produced in America relating the stories of Moors.

GENERAL GORDON

When the Moors civilized Europe, wearing of the fez spread to Turkey and became synonymous with conversion to the Islamic religion. Those who wore the fez were respected and bore the title *Effendi*. **Duse Mohammed Ali**, a teacher of Marcus Garvey, was known as Bey Effendi. Effendi is a title of respect and, in Turkish, equivalent to "sir."

Duse Mohammed Ali (1865-1945 A.D.)

Sir: middle English variant of sire meaning senile senior, elder.

The word effendi was taken from Medieval Greek meaning "master" implying one who has mastered many subjects a complete total man. Knowledgeable; learnt.

The Turks took the fez to Persia, and from there to many other foreign countries. French alteration included the addition of a front brim (visor) to block the sun. In this form, it was worn by the French foreign legion as a part of their military uniform. This influenced all caps worn by police officers and military officers to this day. All uniform headwear take their form from the original faas, fez of the Moors.

The Fez is also called a Tarba, which is much taller than the Fez with a much longer tassel than that worn by the Shriners today. Masonic and Shriner headwear includes a tacked down tassel and is often mistaken for the Fez but not the same headdress. The Tarba was an ancient symbol of Lower Egypt's

ruling class and worn by Nubians such as Mentuhotep (above). You will find that most of the Egyptians knowledge used by Shriners has its origin in Aswan and Nubian. The headdress worn by the Shriners is more in line with the headdress of ancient Egyptian tarbush, as it was called by the Arabs and also adapted it as a crown of nobility. It was usually crimson or black and worn by both male and female.

This statue of Heru/Horus is depicted as a Falcon wearing a fez. George G.M James in *Stolen Legacy* teaches us that the Moors became custodians of Egyptian customs when the Dynasty of KMT fell to foreign powers. Most people mistake the fez for the tarba/ tarboosh due to their similar appearance. Both head wear have a circumference of 360 degrees of spiritual knowledge and 360 degrees of physical knowledge at the bottom equaling 720 degrees.

This is also the Law of Correspondence and the Law of Balance. Both the Fez and the Tarbush are brimless headpieces usually tasseled and made of felt. They represent an Imperial ruler and are symbolic of learning and enlightenment, so leaders and learnt men throughout history have adorned the Tarbush or a Fez. It must be noted that the Fez of Morocco was a city, a great center for learning and was once the northern capital of Morocco. The headpiece bearing the same name is also a symbol of this great city. The Black Fez was the highest degree of nobility worn by the Mufti Staff and the elite councils of the Adept Chambers of the Moorish Science Temple.

Here is a picture of the Moors of Ceylon, modernly called Sri Lanka. They are called today Lankan Moors.

10. The Fez in the MHT of S and MST of A

The body of the Fez represents the Pyramid, but more importantly it is symbolic of the universe we live in, a.k.a. the cosmic womb. At the top of the Fez are four corners of dots and in the middle is where the birth takes place. The top is symbolic of the planet Earth on which we live and the four corners are symbolic of the four breaks in the Circle 7 representing the four seasons, the four major compounds of this planet – Earth, Air, Water, Fire – which is what YHWH really stands for. Inside of the four corners are sets of dots, a circle of nine dots, 12 dots and 18 dots. The nine dots represent the time it takes to gestate in our mother's womb, as well as nine is the number of completion. The 12 dots represent the signs of the zodiac in astrology, in which we all came to the planet representing a multitude of zodiac formations, or what are called the children of Israel, or Jesus disciples. The 18 dots are symbolic of as above so below the cosmic principle of correspondence and gender; male and female which creates one divine being still equaling nine.

The stem which comes from the inside of the top of the fez represents "I," the ninth letter in the alphabet. The stem is connected to a cord that is symbolic of the umbilical cord and is tied to its earthly mother; the mundane circle. This cord that is wrapped around the mundane circle and holds its form is called "the ties of unity" because all things are bound by a cord as well the cyclical and reciprocal nature of life. The strands of the tassels represent 360 degrees of knowledge flowing at 360 degrees and are not tacked down to the fez. As explained earlier, after the fall of Granada, the culture of the Moors was to be wiped from the minds of their descendants, including their Divine, National Intellectual headwear; the fez.

11. Fez-Wearing Imposters

AKA Culture Vultures

Institutionalized graduation in Westernized (not European) societies is marked by receipt of a graduation gown and mortar board. This headwear is supposed to mean you have attained some level of intellect.

To the left is pictured a replica of the fez. Notice the tassel and flattened top, which is four **90** degree angles, which, when added together, equal **360** degrees. Keep in mind, Free Masonry teaches, a diploma is a rolled up piece of paper.

Here is a Thanksgiving menu picture with a European girl wearing the Moors' fez. What does Thanksgiving have to do with the fez?

This picture of an electric chair headpiece requires little examination to see how much it resembles a fez. In this guise, it was used by the imposters was used to take lives to stain this headwear with a bad reputation. The fez is symbolic of the womb and represents the living and growing intellect of the wearer

Even the Nazi's took the fez in order to mislead the masses into submitting to their rule. This was attempted by misusing the power of the fallen Moors through the energy of our National headwear. Behind the swastika, the Nazis represented with the fez of the fallen Moors. Why we never shown these pictures with Nazis wearing the National headdress of the Moors as their military headwear?

Grupa muslimanskih dobrovoljaca iz divizije "Handžar". Svi nose fesove. Oznake su mrtvačka glava i SS orao. Fes su nosili kako vojnici Muslimani tako i njemački oficiri te divizije. Bilo je više modela fesa u različitim bojama (zeleni, crveni, sa ili bez kićanke). Na ovratnicima uniformi utkane su kriva sabija i kukasti križ.

Smotra divizije

HRVATI HERCEG-BOSNE!

**VELIKI VODJE ADOLF HITLER
I POGLAVNIK Dr. ANTE PAVELIĆ
POZIVAJU VAS NA OBRANU VAŠIH OGNJIŠTA
UVRSTITE SE U REDOVE DOBROVOLJAČKIH
HRVATSKIH SS POSTROJBI**

Lord Kitchener
British Army Officer

One of the most well-known wearers of a fez in a Hollywood film was by Victor Mature playing Dr Omar in Josef Von Sternberg's The Shanghai Gesture (1942)

Tommy Cooper was born in Wales on March 19, 1921. Soon after the outbreak of World War II, Cooper joined the army and served for seven years until 1947. For much of this time his regiment was posted to the Middle East. When opportunity allowed he worked on his performances as a failed magician. It was during his time in Cairo that Tommy Cooper got his trademark hat – a Moorish fez

"The Fez is an elegant addition to any gent's wardrobe," says *King Kini, the suave musical matador who reigns over the Club Velvet Cocktail Lounge in downtown Minneapolis. "Its appeal lies in the purity of its design. The way the curves follow the contour of the human*

head... a simple single tassel as decoration... beautiful." Kini, who refuses to reveal much of his past or his real name, is fast-becoming the doyenne of cocktail culture *and also points out, "It's not the LENGTH of the tassel, it's HOW IT HANGS that counts...*

"That Kini is quite a character," says renowned fashion designer Gianni Versace, "I'm not so sure of his musical taste, but he knows headwear and he's right about the fez. (Gordon 1997).

Cartoon "artists" have jacked the fez to make a mockery of it. We Moors were falsely said to have come from monkeys during the time of slavery to justify our being considered as low as beasts. Abu, from the animated film *Aladdin*, represents the Niger; the troglodyte nigger monkey or the melanin being with the mind of a minor, hence black people being called minorities.

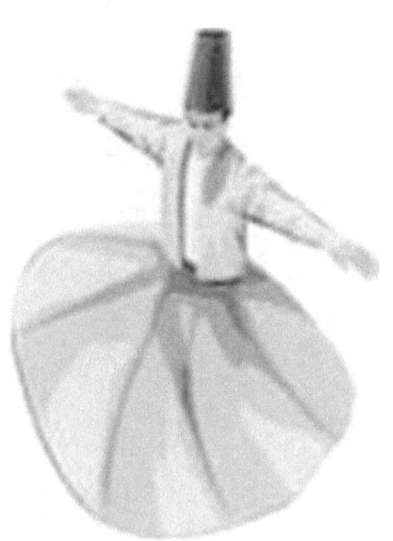

12. Prophet Noble Drew Ali was not a Mason

"I came to take the cover off all secret societies."

Many of the inept who are severely and emotionally attached to one school of thought BELIEVE Prophet Noble Drew Ali is a nigger, a self-proclaimed Prophet and a mason. Unconscious Moors and more so the ignorant and blinded ones never see the full picture unless it's brought to them. Many internet fanatics who use YouTube, MySpace, FaceBook, etc., as tools to reach masses, resort to slander in order to gain popularity among those ignoramus cadavers seeking some kind of hope or change outside themselves. The Prophet taught us that opinion is fine, but is no proof of truth. Many fail to build with ones who are in the know and these ones really believe their no-proof opinions are facts. In the face of truth they tend to turn from it and or completely ignore it.

Free masons take an oath to not reveal those secret teachings revealed behind the closed doors of the lodges. The "oath of death" silences the mason after he leaves the lodge. Masons are so secret about their rituals they cannot even wear their fez outside the lodge. In our Oral Statements of Prophet Noble Drew Ali booklet, statement #144, he says, "I took the cover of all secret organizations". Many see this as meaning he was part of the secret organizations and was revealing what was hidden there. Truth be told, Noble Drew Ali was teaching Moors and anyone willing to hear his message that the lodges were in possession of the Birthright of the Moors and that it was time for us to reclaim our lost culture. It is taught that Master Teachers like Ben Banneker Bey taught the European Masons about government and the Egyptian high science before its fall to foreign invaders.

When we look at Masonic names and symbols we must ask, how did Europeans, who were Neanderthals, get a hold of these customs that were not theirs? Where did they get the star, crescent and scimitar? The crescent and star are Islamic symbols and free masons like Shriners etc. are not Moslems. Why is the head of a wombman with Egyptian headwear on their crest when they were not Egyptian? With an open mind you can clearly see that these are stolen/confiscated symbols of the Moors who fell in 1492.

> *"The salutation among the Faithful is "Es Selamu Aleikum!" This means "Peace be with You!" In returning the salutation, the gracious wish is "Aleikum es Selamu" "With you be peace."* (Jamil Shrine Temple n.d.)

Does his sound familiar to you, I hear Muslims say this salutation all the time but Masons aren't Muslims!!!!!

Much of what the Prophet did SEEMS to resemble freemasonry but the fact remains that the Prophet was a Egyptian Adept, meaning he mastered more degrees, 720, that any mason and would be over qualified for the lodge if he was a mason.

> *"Noble drew Ali was not a freemason. For all those who have ever made that claim, notice, they never produce a dues card, travel card, ledger, lodge name or any other freemasonic documents with Drew Ali's name on it."* (Muhammad al-Mahdi 1998).

It is said that the temple was overrun by Moors in fezzes who were Free Masons in disguise. Due to their oath, they were compelled to attempt a burial of Noble Drew Ali and the Moorish Movement so as to forever keep Hiram Abiff from rising from his shallow grave.

> *"The fez, which Nobles of the Mystic Shrine of North America have the privilege and honor of wearing, has been handed down through the ages as one of the most significant of all headdresses. "* (Jamil Shrine Temple n.d.)

Now, based on the evidence presented herein, who do you think handed down the fez and bestowed the privilege and honour to Free Masons and Shriners wearing it today? Without doubt or contradiction; the Moors.

Works Cited

Altabe, David Fintz. "The Significance of 1492 to the Jews and Muslims of Spain." *Hispania*, 1992: 728-731.

Bey, C.M. *Clock of Destinty*. Vol. II. Clock of Destiny International Order of the Great Seal, n.d.

Dixon, Roland Burrage. *Racial History of Man*. New York: Charles Scribner's Sons, 1923.

Gordon, S. "Headwear of the Millennium?" *Club Velvet*. May 5, 1997. http://www.tamboo.com/clubvelvet/time/index.html (accessed Jan 22, 2015).

Hacienda Home Style. "Spanish Ironworks Moorish Influence." *Hacienda Home Style*. 2008. http://haciendahomestyle.com/spanish-ironworks-Moorish-influence/ (accessed Jan 22, 2015).

James, George G.M. *Stolen Legacy: Greek Philosophy is Stolen Egyptian Philosophy* . Trenton, NJ: Africa World Press, 1992.

Jamil Shrine Temple. *Shrine History*. n.d. http://www.jamilshriners.com/historyoftheshrine.html (accessed Jan 22, 2015).

Laliberte, G.-Raymond. "Secret Societies." *The Canadian Encyclopedia*. Feb 7, 2006. http://www.thecanadianencyclopedia.com/en/article/secret-societies/ (accessed Jan 21, 2015).

Muhammad al-Mahdi, Isa Abd Allah. *Who Was Noble Drew Ali*.

Eatonton, GA: Ansaru Allah Community, 1998.

Noble Drew Ali, Prophet. *The Holy Koran of the Moorish Science Temple of America Circle 7.* Chicago: Moorish Guide Publishing, 1928.

Roynayne, Edmond. "Roynanye's Hand Book of Freemasonry: A Comple." *Phoenix Masonry.* June 2007. http://www.phoenixmasonry.org/roynaynes_handbook_of_freemasonry.htm (accessed Jan 21, 2015).

Tannenbaum, Frank. *Slave and Citizen: The Classic Comparative Study of Race Relations in the Americas.* Boston: Beacon Press, 1992.

Teixeira dos Santos M.M., Marcio. "Symbolism of the Third Degree." *MasonicWorld.ocm.* n.d. http://www.masonicworld.com/education/files/oct03/symbolism_of_the_third_degree__i.htm (accessed Jan 21, 2015).

Index

Al-Andalus, 12
Alpujarra Uprising, 15
Aurora Grata Consistory, 3
ben Abu, Diego Lopez, 15
ben Ferag, Ferag, 15
Boaz, 9
Byzantine Empire, 17
Canadaigwa, 23
Chakras, 4
Constantinople, 17
Effendi, 24
Entered Apprentice, 4, 7
Fell Spirits, 14
Fellow Craft, 4
Fellow-craft, 7
Fleming, Walter M., 3
Florence, Willim J., 3
Hiram Abiff, 5, 6
Ibn Ibi Talib, Ali, 3
Kara, 17
Khent, 23

Khmer Empire, 20
Knights Templar, 3
Kwesi, Ashra, 5
Lion Paw, 7
Malachizodok El, 5
Master Mason, 4
Master Potentates, 6
Morisco Revolt, 15
Mufti, 26
Muslim League, The, 18
Nazi, 30
Order of Quetzalcoatl, The, 4
Osman I, 17
peci, 21
Phillip II, 15
serpentine fire, 20
Sultan Bayazid II, 14
Tarba, 24
Tarbush, 18
Timbuktu, 23
Torquemada, Tomas, 14

Other Titles Available from Califa Media®

Moorish Children's Guide to History and Culture

Moorish Jewels: Emerald Ed

Moors in America

Moslem Girls' Training Guide a.k.a. The Sisters' Auxiliary Handbook

Nationality, the Order of the Day

Noble Drew Ali Plenipotentiaries

Official Proclamation of Real Moorish American Nationality

Well, Come to Klanada

Califa Uhuru Series

Vol. 1:   Holy Koran of the Moorish Holy Temple of Science, Circle 7

Vol. 2: "I'm Going to Repeat Myself.":   A Collection of Artifacts Authored by Noble Prophet Drew Ali and the M.S.T. of A.

Vol. 3:   Mysteries of the Silent Brotherhood of the East a.ka. The Red Book, a.k.a. Sincerity

Vol. 4:   Califa Uhuru; A Collection of Literature from the Moorish Science Temple of America

www.ingramcontent.com/pod-product-compliance
Lightning Source LLC
Chambersburg PA
CBHW030202100526
44592CB00009B/406